T0157827

POSTCODE

POSTCODE

Exploring the Secret Place of God

Modupe Afolabi

authorHOUSE®

AuthorHouse™
1663 Liberty Drive
Bloomington, IN 47403
www.authorhouse.com
Phone: 1-800-839-8640

First published by AuthorHouse   05/16/2011

ISBN: 978-1-4567-7923-8 (sc)
ISBN: 978-1-4567-7937-5 (ebk)

Printed in the United States of America

Introduction

People often think they know God but the question is, do they really know Him? Do you know God? Do I know God? These questions may appear personal and, to some, intrusive, but I believe that no Christian has come to maturity until such a person is able to ask himself, "Do I know God, at least the way I should?" and then sincerely come up with an accurate but honest assessment of self as it relates to the knowledge of God.

If Moses could still ask to experience God in another dimension then he already had, even after those wonderful encounters and his fellowship with God (Exodus, 33:13-23), then you and I can do no less. God, Himself, bore witness to Moses' knowledge of the Godhead when He aided Aaron and Miriam. *"With him [Moses] will I speak mouth to mouth . . ." (Numbers 12:8),* and yet Moses considered himself not to have comprehended God. What a lesson!

In the New Testament, we see something similar to that of Moses in Paul, the Apostle. Paul once said, *"Brethren, I count not myself to have posessed it: but this one thing I do . . . I press toward the mark for the prize of the high calling of God in Christ Jesus" (Philippians, 3:13-14). And what is the aim? ". . . that I may know Him and the power of His resurrection, and the fellowship of His sufferings, being made conformable unto His death . . ." (Philippians 3:10).* And that was the Paul who had abundance of revelations of God and from God!

Oh! How we need such people and mentality today. *"Let us therefore, as many as would be perfect, be thus minded," Paul concluded (Philippians, 3:15).* I believe that Christians of today have lots to learn from this great Apostle of God in regard to knowing God.

Paul, in writing to the church in Corinth, said, *'Examine yourselves whether ye be in the faith. Prove you own selves.' (2 Corinthians, 13:5a).*

Self-assessment and examination is something very important in one's walk as a Christian. It is a vital part of human progress and development, but the thing is that it is largely neglected by so many. It is a great virtue in the Christian faith and God esteems it highly in His dealings with us. In fact, look through the pages of the scriptures: it looks as if whenever any man judges or examines or assesses himself, mercy always triumphs over divine judgement (James, 2:13). As a matter of fact, in Psalms 51, that was what God saw and was endeared to David.

Now, why all the above statements and illustrations on the subject of self-examination and the knowledge of God? One of the areas where Christians must thoroughly and sincerely examine themselves is in the area of their knowledge and acquaintance with God.

How truly do you know God? Yes, you have you heard of God, you might even believe and 'know' Him, but do you know where He dwells? Where is God's home address if I may ask you? And assuming you know it, have you been there? Do you live there? Are you a regular caller as far as God's abode is concerned? Or, are you the on-and-off type?

Before the beginning and since the creation of all things, God has always had a dwelling place. Even though God is everywhere, omnipresent as we call it, He still has an abode. I think the best way to explain and describe God's omnipresence is to say: God sits on His throne in Heaven and His eyes see EVERYTHING under the sun. He is on His throne in Heaven but at the same time His eyes are in every place (Proverbs, 15:3). And when He chooses to practically make His presence known, He shows up in any particular place.

The above, to me, is the best way of describing God's omnipresent nature so that man doesn't lose the truth of the fact that God has a dwelling—a postcode.

There is a dwelling place called the 'Secret Place' which is where our God dwells and the pages of scripture are full of invitations to humanity to come and dwell there with God. This is the reason for this book. This book is an exploration into the Secret Place of God. It is a call to all, especially those who have a saving knowledge of God to make God's dwelling place their own. It is also to reveal to you the benefits you stand to gain by living in His presence.

God has never sent anyone who wants to dwell with Him away. In fact, it is God's desire that we all live where he dwells. He desires it. He longs for it but it all depends on us. How willing are you and how desirous are you for His presence? One thing is sure though, if you desire it, God will see to it that you see the reality of it. Regarding the willingness of God to bring us to His dwelling place, a very interesting passage is found in the book of Saint John, chapter 1 that shows it very clearly, but that is, of course, only if you crave for it:

> *"Again the next day after John stood, with two of his disciples; and looking upon Jesus as he walked, he saith, "Behold the Lamb of God!" And the two disciples heard him speak, and they followed Jesus. Then Jesus turned, and saw them following, and said unto them; 'What seek ye?' They said unto him, 'Rabbi, [which is to say, being interpreted, Master], where dwellest thou?'*
>
> *He saith unto them, "Come and see." They came and saw where he dwelt and abode with him that day: for it was about the tenth hour." (John 1:35-39)*

In the above scripture, John's disciples (two of them) asked the Lord, Where dwellest thou? And what was Jesus' reply?

'Come and see'. And they both went and abode with him that day. What an insight about how willing God is to see us in his abode! And you might ask, how?

John 1:18 says, *"No man hath seen God at any time; the only begotton Son, which is the bosom of the Father, He hath declared [revealed] Him."* That is, if there is anything anyone wants to learn or know about God, let such a person look to Jesus. If Jesus did it, if Jesus said it, then that is exactly what God will say and or do. How Jesus responded is how God will respond.

Therefore, going back to John 1:35-39, the way Jesus responded clearly shows how God wants to respond. Jesus did not hesitate or refuse the desires of the two disciples of John to come and know where he lives. So likewise, God is willing to take them to His dwelling place.

God is more willing than we are concerning living within His Secret Place. He longs for us. Like Jesus, He is saying to you right now, come and see where I dwell. He wants it, but do you?

How willing are you? How much of God's dwelling place do you crave? The message of this book is this: You don't know God until you know and become acquinted with His dwelling place.

It is in His dwelling place that we all come to know Him better. It is our fellowship with Him in His dwelling place that makes us more like Him.

> *'He that dwelleth in the secret place of the Most High shall abide under the shadow of the Almighty.' (Psalm 91:1).*

God has a dwelling place. God has a postcode and it is as declared above. How familiar is this place to you? Have you been there? Do you live there or are you just a squatter there?

Chapter 1

God's Secret Place

Where does God dwell? Where does God live? In Heaven? Yes. On earth? Oh yes! For the bible says His footstool is the earth (Isaiah, 66:1). Where does God dwell? Everywhere? Again, yes. But is the above the answer? NO. Why? Because the scriptures make us understand that God's dwelling place is a Secret Place.

That is, even though He dwells in Heaven and He is everywhere, His place of abode is still a secret! How? It is hidden but only known to a few. Why? Because it requires certain conditions to be met before anyone can have access to it. In this chapter we shall be looking into the Word to see what it teaches concerning this subject of the Secret Place of God.

In teaching the popular Lord's Prayer, the Lord Jesus clearly confirms the truth that our God dwells in the Secret Place:

> *"But thou, when thou prayest, enter into thy closet, and when thou hast shut thy door, pray to thy Father who is in secret; and thy Father who seeth in secret shall reward thee openly."* (Matthew, 6:6)

From the above, it is clear that our God dwells in the Secret Place. The Father we pray to is in <u>secret</u> according to the Lord. First, it is Jesus who has been in the bosom of the Father in Heaven before coming to the earth who said and revealed it.

And, according to John 1:18, whatever Jesus tells us is firsthand information which anyone can rely on. So, you and I can rest assured that the Lord Jesus knows what he was saying by the words spoken in Matthew 6:6 without mixing words.

Second, from what the Lord reveals in Matthew 6:6, one can notice useful truth about God's Secret Place: "When thou prayest, enter into <u>thy closet</u>, and when thou hast <u>shut thy door</u>, pray to thy Father which is in <u>secret</u>." This means that even though God dwells in the Secret Place, He can still be revealed in the simplest and easiest way. How? <u>In thy closet</u> once the <u>door is shut</u>. That is, even though God is 'hidden', He is not far from any of us. In other words, if you can at any time <u>shut</u> yourself up in your <u>closet</u>, away from all the distractions of life, God can be accessed and reached.

What a simple way it is that the Lord has revealed the Secret Place of God to us in those words in Matthew 6:6. So, the puzzle that has kept many away from knowing God's Secret Place has finally been shown by the Lord. It is really not as hard as many think. Why? Because God's Secret Place is all around us, waiting for the ones who will take that extra step of locking themselves away'. That extra step of separation. That extra step of shutting oneself up from the busy atmosphere of life into the closet where God dwells.

It is simple: God's Secret Place is only dependent on how willing and ready each one of us is. And, as long as you are ready to shut yourself up from the world, either in spirit or in a physical way, God can be accessed.

Paul, the Apostle, once said, God is not far from everyone of us: *'For in Him we live, and move, and have our being' (Acts, 17:28).* God is as close to you as your skin and activities. If we put it another way, God's Secret Place is there with you and around you, even in your house, only waiting to be made a reality by your own personal conscious act of exclusion from all others. This is the simplest it can ever be, as the Lord revealed in Matthew 6:6.

Therefore, where does God dwell if I may ask you again? I know you know what the answer is! <u>In your closet</u>. God is as close as you are to yourself. That's right! God's Secret Place is in 'thy closet'. God is right there where you are.

> *"And, lo, I am with you alway, even unto the end of the world."* (Matthew, 28:20b)

The Secret Place of God is in His presence and if you are God's child, God's presence is right there where you are.

The Power of the Closet

> *"For as I passed by and beheld your devotions, I found an alter with this inscription: 'To The Unknown God'. Whom therefore ye worship in ignorance, Him I declare unto you. God who made the world and all things therein, seeing that he is Lord of Heaven and earth, dwelleth not in*

> *temples made with hands. Neither is worshipped with men's hands. He hath made of one blood all nations of men and caused them to dwell on all the face of the earth . . . that they should seek the Lord, if perhaps they might feel after Him, and find Him, though he be not far from any one of us. For in Him we live, and move, and have our being . . ."* (Acts, 17:23-28).

Reading the above, you will notice one thing stands out which I have already shown you: God who made the heavens and the earth <u>is not far from any one of us</u> because we are his offspring, (verses 27 and 28).

God is not far from you. We live in Him, we move in Him, and, in fact, in Him we have our being. God is closer than any mortal man can ever be to you. What is the power of the closet? It is the very fact that the closet to any one of us is God. And the only reason why we have not come to the realisation of this all important truth of the Word is we have all made it hard for ourselves to believe, and many are in ignorance of it.

Ignorance of this truth is the biggest problem and hindrance to a glorious path and relationship with God. And what is this truth? That God is all around us. The Word, which is God (1 John, 1-3), made this world and thus God could not be very far from us. He is much closer to us than we can ever imagine. Man has only kept divinity distant by the unwillingness to unlock the doors of the closet.

We hold the key to the closet. We have reluctantly refused to put the key into the key hole. We have refused to open the door that leads to the closet. We have kept ourselves distant from Him. Why? Because His position never changes, it is we who have drawn ourselves further away from Him.

What is the power of the closet? It is because that is where God dwells. *'And Jacob was left alone; and there wrestled a man with him until the breaking of the day . . .And*

Jacob called the name of the place, Peniel: [that is The face of God] 'For I have seen God face to face and my life is preserved." (Genesis, 32: 24, 38). In the <u>closest</u>, even through an open field, Jacob met with God because he was left <u>alone</u>. The power of the closet is because God dwells there and is found there and nowhere else.

What is the power of the closet? It is because ONLY God sees us in the closet. It is an interaction with divinity. In the closet, no man can be seen there but you alone, and I mean no matter if there is a crowd around you. The power of the closet is that God alone see it:

> *"Whither shall I go from thy spirit? Or whither shall I flee from thy presence? If I ascend up into heaven, thou art there: if I make my bed in hell, behold Thou art there.If I take the wings of the morning and dwell in thr uttermost parts of the sea, even there shall Thy hand lead me, and Thy right hand shall hold me. If I say,*

*"Surely the darkness shall cover me"
even the night shall be light about me.
Yea, the darkness hideth not from thee;
but the night shineth as the day; the
darkness and the light are both alike
to Thee"* (Psalms, 139:7-12).

Nothing can be a hindrance to God as the closet is concerned. If you make the appointment to be with Him in the closet, there you will find Him. In your closet, in spirit or in a physical sense, once you have been able to turn off from the world and are turned to God, you can always be assured that God will be found, simply because He is always there.

The Secret Place of God is not a matter of a geographical location but a reflection of the presence of God. God sees everywhere and everything, and has the power to physically manifest to a conscious seeker.

The words of the Psalm we just read said; "And the answer is that thou art there." Where? Anywhere I am found and I think nobody can actually harness the secret, the

Secret Place of God until such is able to see the power it carries.

God's Secret Place carries power and that power lies in our understanding and revelation of the personality of God: His own omnipresent and omniscient nature. If you know God can be found in your bedroom, you will not find it difficult reaching out to Him. If you know God is the 'all knowing', 'all seeing' and present everywhere at the same time, then you will realise that the very moment you shut your doors to appear before Him, He is already there waiting for you. The power of the closet and the understanding of the same is what opens anyone up to an unending exploration with God.

It Requires an Act

> *"Draw nigh to God, and he will draw nigh to you."*
> (James, 4:8a)

"And in the morning, rising up a great while before day; He [Jesus] went out, and departed into <u>a solitary place</u>, and there prayed." (Mark, 1:35).

One sincere truth is this, the Secret Place of God which anyone of us can access through the closet, can only be achieved by a conscious act of will. It doesn't come by wishing but it requires a conscious effort. Nobody will take you or I to the closet. Even when people succeed in taking you there, nobody will create a closet for you. And it is called a closet because no one else, no matter how many are around you, can be there with you. It is a personal appointment and contact with God.

Do you know why it is called God's Secret Place? Because you and I are there 'secretly'. No one else can be involved in the process but you. If you don't draw yourself near God, He will not draw Himself near to you either (James, 4:8a). But why? It is because *"God is a spirit, and they that worship Him must worship Him in spirit and in truth." (John, 4:24)*

It takes the spirit of a man to be in God's presence and to interact with Him. And this is where many are missing. But why is that? Because it is very possible to be physically present but miles away from the Secret Place.

So, the act of a man's will is where the serious work begins. and this is what James 4:8a reveals. God is spirit and so until your spirit is consciously drawn towards God, the closet that is supposed to be a place of meeting with God may remain like any other ordinary place.

Do you want to be in God's presence as you enter into your closet? Then consciously and seriously with the act of your human spirit, shut yourself off from the busy life and atmosphere around you. Close the door behind you, as seen in Matthew 6:6, and God will be right there before you.

To help you define what the closet is, I will show you scriptural descriptions of the closet:

Various Closets

1. Your heart

"My son, give me thine heart."
(Proverbs, 23:26a)

". . . but the Lord looketh on the heart." 1 Samuel, 16:7c)

"And ye shall seek Me, and find Me, <u>when</u> ye shall search for Me with all your heart." (Jeremiah, 29:13)

". . . and I will cause him to draw near, and he shall approach unto me: for who is this that engaged his heart to approach unto Me? saith the Lord. And ye shall be my people, and I will be your God." (Jeremiah, 30:21b-22)

"And whatsoever ye do, <u>do it heartily . . .</u>"
(Colossians, 3:23)

"Behold, I stand at the door and knock: if any man hear my voice, and open the door, I will come in to him, and will sup with him, and he with me."
(Revelation, 3:20)

2. Your bedroom

"But thou, when thou prayest, <u>enter into thy closet</u> [bedroom], and when thou hast <u>shut thy door</u>, pray to thy Father who is in secret, and thy Father who seeth in secret shall reward thee openly." (Matthew, 6:6)

3. Any Moment of Acknowledgment

"Draw nigh to God, and he will draw nigh to you." (James, 4:8a)

"The Lord is nigh unto all them that call upon Him, to all that call upon Him in truth." (Psalms,145:18)

4. The Gathering in His Name

"Again I say unto you, that if two of you shall agree on earth as concerning anything that they shall ask, it shall be done for them of My Father which is in Heaven. For where two or three are gathered together in My name, there am I in the midst of them."
(Matthew, 18:19-20)

"Teaching them to observe all things whatsoever I have commanded you: and, lo, I am with you always, even unto the end of the world."
(Matthew, 28: 20)

Chapter 2

The Man Who Dwells with God

Since God's dwelling place is a Secret Place, it means that not everybody will be able to access it. But note that everybody has the invitation to enter it; however, there *are* conditions. Just like there are dress codes to certain events or pastors so that even though you may be invited, it is not until you adhere to the dress code that you are allowed in, so is the case with God's dwelling place.

Also note that because it is called the 'Secret Place' of God, it means that only members of the 'fraternity' can go in. So, who is the man that dwells in God's Secret Place? Who can gain access and enter into His Secret Place?

> *"Lord, who shall abide in Thy tabernacle? Who shall dwell in thy holy hill? He that walketh uprightly and worketh righteousness, and speaketh the truth in his heart; he that backbiteth not with his tongue, nor doeth evil to his neighbour, nor taketh up a reproach against his neighbour. In whose eyes a vile person is contemned; but he honoureth them that fear the Lord. He that taketh an oath to his own hurt, and changeth not; he that putteth not out his money to usury, nor taketh a bribe against the innocent. He that doeth these things shall never be moved."* (Psalms, 15:1-5)

A big list isn't it? But that is the condition that has to be fulfilled before anyone can gain entrance to God's holy hill. A quick summary according to Psalm is righteousness, purity or holiness of life and character.

But where does it all begin? Will any man say because he is pure and without any reproach that he can dwell with God? Can the morally clean person claim the right to God's Secret Place? The answer is no. It takes more than self-righteousness to dwell with God, otherwise even the moralist will be God's co-tenants. Where does it all begin then?

1. <u>Salvation: New Birth</u>

The man who dwells with God would have confessed his sins and had his life washed by the blood of Jesus as an initial step, otherwise all other conditions, even when met, will not be recognised by God.

> *"But as many as received Him [Jesus], to them gave He [God] power to become the sons of God, even to those who believe in His Name, who were born, not of blood, nor of the will of the flesh, nor of the will of man, <u>but of God</u>."* (John 1:12-13)

How?

> *"Whosoever believeth that Jesus is the Christ is born of God . . ."* (1 John, 5:1)

> *"That if thou shall confess with thy mouth the Lord Jesus, and shalt believe in thine heart that God hath raised Him from the dead, thou shalt be saved. For with the heart man believeth unto righteousness, and with the mouth confession is made unto salvation."* (Romans, 10:9-10)

Why?

> *"For all have sinned, and come short of the glory of God." (Romans 3:23)*

> *". . . And all our righteousness are as filthy rags . . ."* (Isaiah, 64:6)

And even when you think you are 'clean' as a human being, that is, morally upright, what of the Adamic sin which was passed unto all men?

> *"Wherefore, as by one man sin entered into the world, and death by sin; and so death passed upon all men, for that all have sinned."* (Romans, 5:12).

So, any way you look at it, to dwell in God's presence, salvation through Christ is required and faith in the same must be met (John, 3:16 and Ephesians, 2:8). Therefore, until a man has received Jesus Christ as Lord and Saviour by faith in his atonement and towards God, no access to God's Secret

Place can be granted. Redemption is the first step.

Now, when a man has fulfilled the salvation question, will he then fold his hands and relax? No, of course not!

2. Sin Issues

> *"If I regard iniquity in my heart, the Lord will not hear me."* (Psalms, 66:18)

> *"Thou art of purer eyes than to behold evil, and canst not look on iniquity . . ."* (Habakkuk, 1:13)

If any man is to dwell with God then such must not be a lover of sin. The word 'regard' used in Psalms 66:18 is translated to 'cherish' in other Bible translations.

Those who cherish and have respect for sin or place value on sin will never be able to dwell with God. Didn't you see the words of Habakkuk 1:13? God's eyes are purer that to behold evil neither can look upon iniquity. You cannot go before God with sin and expect Him to let you in. Psalms 15:1-2 says it is only the righteous who will be able to dwell with the Lord.

> *"If ye know that He is righteous, ye know that every one that <u>doeth</u> righteousness is born of Him."* (1John, 2:29)

> *"Whosoever is born of God doth not commit sin."* (1 John, 3:9a)

> *"Behold, the arm of the Lord is not too short to save, neither his ear heavy, that it cannot hear: but your iniquities have <u>separated you from your God</u>, your sins have <u>hidden his face from you</u>, so that he will not hear."* (Isaiah, 59:1-2)

That says it all doesn't it? Sin and iniquity will separate a man from God. Where there is sin, God hides Himself from men. Sin will keep God in His Secret Place and close the doors behind Him so that no man can go in. Therefore, the antidote is this: do you want to dwell with God? Then keep sin away.

Having therefore seen what sin can do to a man who wants to dwell with God, what then is the way forward? The answer is this:

3. <u>The Man Who Dwells with God Knows How to Confess his Sins</u>

"If we confess our sins, He is faithful and just to forgive us our sins, and cleanse us from all unrighteousness." (1 John, 1:9)

The only way to deal with sin is to confess and forsake it. And so, those who do not know how to confess their sins in a most specific way cannot enjoy the Secret Place of God.

"Blessed is he whose transgressions are forgiven . . . when I kept silence, my

bones grew old through my groaning all the day long. For day and night Thy hand was heavy upon me; the sap of my soul was turned into the drought of summer. I <u>acknowledge my sin unto Thee</u>, and mine iniquity have I hid not. I said, "<u>I will confess my transgressions unto the Lord</u>; and Thou forgavest the iniquity of my sin. For this shall everyone that is godly pray unto Thee in a time when Yhou mayest be found; surely in the floods of great waters shall not come nigh unto him." (Psalms, 32:1-6)

Those who keep silent when they have a sin to confess will never know peace. They will lose the privilege that is theirs in Christ, and above all will lose their place in the Secret Place.

Verse 3 of Psalm 32 above says, "When I kept silent, my bones waxed old through my roaring all the day long." Can you imagine that? Keeping quiet when you should have confessed places you on the same side as the devil: "roaring all the day long" like the devil does according to Peter 1, 5:8, it describes the devil roaring to and fro on the earth. I doubt you would want to have the same status as the devil?

Therefore, the earlier you confess your sins, the better. Sincerely, it is dangerous to keep quiet when there is a sin to confess. And, at least, if there is anything that should compel anyone to reach out to God in confession, it should be the risking of the Secret Place of God. You don't want to lose it all just because you refuse to confess your sins.

And to confess is not all there is to it. You must also be ready to forsake the confessed sin: *"He that covereth his sins shall not prosper: but who so <u>confesseth and forsaketh</u> them shall have mercy." (Proverbs, 28:13).*

To conclude, let me say it again, not confessing your sins is dangerous. It can cast you away from the Secret Place: "Cast me not away from thy presence and take not thy Holy Spirit from me," was what David said in Psalm 51:11; he had sinned against God for his adultery with Bathsheba who was the wife of Uriah (2 Samuel, 11).

A sin not confessed can cast a man away from the Secret Place. Therefore, the man who must dwell in the Secret Place must know how to deal with sin. And how is that? By confession!

4. Good Human Relation

The man who dwells with God has a good relationship with others. He feels no resentment against anyone in his heart. He is a lover of people:

> *"If a man say, "I love God" and hateth his brother, he is a liar. For he that loveth not his brother whom he hath seen, how can he love God who he hath not seen? And this commandment have we from Him, that he that loveth God love his brother also."* (1 John, 4:20-21)

It takes love to live with God like we see in John 14:21-23, but such love will not be acceptable by God if it is not extended to others around you, if you say you love God then you must love the man you see also.

If you cannot love men and have good fellowship with the man you see, you certainly cannot have a fellowship with God and you cannot dwell in His presence.

> *"Therefore, if thou bring thy gift to the altar, and there rememberest that thy brother hath ought against thee, leave there thy gift before the altar and go thy way. First be reconciled to thy brother and then come and offer thy gift."* (Matthew, 5:23-24)

So then, what is the first thing a man who wants to dwell in God's Secret Place must do? Quite simply, reconcile with his brother.

5. <u>The Man who Dwells with God is God's Errand Boy</u>

If you are not willing to be an errand boy for the Lord then you cannot live with Him in His Secret Place. And the reason is so simple and straight forward: if God is your Heavenly Father according to scriptures and you are living with Him, who should do the errands, you or the Father?

So, to dwell with God simply means you are ready to do His will, it means that you are ready to be completely obedient to Him.

Using the story of Elijah 1 Kings 17:1-3 as an example, the man who dwells with God:

1. Is God's oracle. He speaks for God
2. Is led by God and not by himself
3. Runs errands for God
4. Is obedient to God
5. Knows how to listen to God
6. Stands before God

7. He understands the moves of God
8. Knows what God's next agenda is

And the summary of it all is this: be obedient to God. Whatever good works he reads or finds in the Bible, he does. And whatever God tells him he does.

Chapter 3

Developing a Lifestyle for His Presence

You and I know that dwelling in God's presence is a lifelong journey and to keep ourselves there we need to develop and possess a lifestyle for it. It requires character to remain there. In this chapter, we shall be looking at the character or lifestyle that anyone who wants to live in God's Secret Place needs to have.

In order to bring this in the right perspective, there are three areas anyone wanting to develop a lifestyle that will promote an onward trend in this subject of God's Secret Place must have. An understanding of these three areas will foster your growth in God.

1. See God as a Father

The Fatherhood of God is one of the greatest secrets of the Christian faith. Why is that so? Because by it anyone of us can become a son to Him. In fact this is the first transformation that happens at the new birth: *"But as many as received him [Jesus], to them gave He power to become the sons of God even to those that believe in His Name . . ." (John, 1:12).*

We become God's children the very moment we welcome Jesus into our hearts. This is indeed amazing, yet many tend to forget this great truth. If you want to do well as a Christian and have the privilege to dwell in the Secret Place, then you must come to terms with the truth that you are God's child, *"For ye have not received the spirit of bondage again to fear, but ye have received the spirit of adoption, whereby we cry "Abba!" "Father"! The spirit itself beareth witness with our spirit, that we are the children of God . . ." (Romans, 8:15-16).*

If you have received Jesus into your life and heart as your Lord and Saviour, then you are God's child. God adopted you into His family by the blood of Jesus (1 Corinthians, 6:19-20) and Peter, 1:18-19). And when do you decide when you want to be God's child? Today of course!

"Behold, what manner of love the Father hath bestowed upon us, that we should be called the sons of God . . . Beloved, now are we the sons of God, and it doth not yet appear what we shall be; but we know that when He shall appear, we shall be like Him, for we shall see Him as He is." (1 John, 3:1-2)

It is therefore upon the above knowledge that all quest for the secret should be built on: God is your Father and you are God's child. Do not let anything rob you of this understanding. If anyone wants to make onward progress in the school of His Secret Place, the first place to begin is adoption into God's family through Jesus Christ as a child. And once this saving faith has been released into your heart according to Romans 12:3, what you do with it on a daily basis as a lifestyle is up to you. It will also go a long way to determine what your progress in the Secret Place will be like.

If you know God as your Heavenly Father and become established in it, you will find it becomes an easy lifestyle and will feel desire in your heart to want to draw nearer to Him. You would also want to spend time fellowshipping in His presence.

Those who know God as their Father have no fear. Those who know God as their Father don't see anything that will ever keep them away from Him. Those who know God as their Father will go a long way to understand the Father's heart of God concerning them.

They know that the Father is ever waiting to receive them to His bosom any time and any day. This was the reason for the parable of the Prodigal Son in Luke 15:11-32. Even while the prodigal son was long gone, the father felt compassion as he desperately waited for him.

2. Know God as a Father

If you don't know God as a Father then you will always run away from Him even when there is no need to run. From His creation God has always gone after man. Genesis 3:8-11, *"They [Adam and Eve] heard the voice of the Lord God walking in the garden in the cool of the day. And Adam and his wife hid themselves from the presence of the Lord God amongst the trees of the garden. And the Lord God called unto Adam, and said unto him, where art thou?"*

Isn't this a wonderful picture to imagine? That even when God knew they had sinned against Him, He still went to look for them. We also see this wonderful nature in our Lord Jesus Christ as recorded in John, chapter 21. The Lord had resurrected and shown himself to the disciples and yet Peter still led a rebellion and went back fishing with the others. But when the Lord met them, he lovingly prepared dinner for them.

Also, in John we see the woman who was caught in adultery, what did Jesus say to her? *". . . neither do I condemn thee; go and sin no more,"* (John, 8:11), was his answer.

Forgiveness is all over the pages of the scriptures and God commands us to do the same. Why? Because His nature is to forgive no matter what it is:

> *"But there is forgiveness with Thee, that Thou mayest be feared."* (Psalms, 130:4)

> *"Bless the Lord, O my soul: and all that is within me, bless His holy*

name . . . Who forgiveth all thine iniquities . . . For as the heaven is high above the earth so great is His mercy toward them that fear Him . . ." (Psalms, 103:1-14)

Knowing God as the mighty forgiver is one character anyone who wants to dwell with Him must have. Let nothing drive you away from God. No matter the fear, the secrets or hidden sins, if you know how to approach God as the forgiver you will go a long way in your walk in the Secret Place. And of a truth, had Judas Iscariot known God as his forgiver, he would not have gone the way he went.

Many people today cannot lift up their heads and look at God because they don't know Him as the forgiver. Many people today have also lost their confidence that has great recompense of reward because they don't know God as their forgiver. Many cannot even forgive themselves because they think God can never forgive them. Why? Because they don't know God as their forgiver.

All these are the lives of the devil. Know that God is a forgiver and it is His nature to forgive. Relate with Him in this dimension and you shall experience a new dimension in your walk with them.

> *"And he arose, and came to his father. But when he was yet a great way off, his father saw him and had compassion, and ran and fell on his neck and kissed him."* (Luke, 15: 20)

3. Develop a Friendship with God

It is not enough to know God as a Father and a forgiver, go further—the place to go to is in your friendship with Him. Know God as a friend. Can God become a man's friend? Oh yes!

> *"And the scripture was fulfilled which saith, "Abraham believed God, and it was imputed unto him for*

righteousness"; and he was called the friend of God."
(James, 2:23)

If you think that is in the Old Testament, then hear what Jesus said to his disciples:

"Greater love hath no man than this, that a man lay down his life for his friends. Ye are My friends, if ye do whatsoever I command you." (John, 15:13-14)

It is very possible to become best of friends with God. And this should be the ultimate goal of everyone seeking the Secret Place of God as a dwelling place. You don't want to relate with Him only as a Father, neither do you want to know Him as a forgiver only. Knowing God as a friend has great blessings too.

Why is that so? Because if someone is your friend, you can ask just about anything of them. For a stranger one can be courteous and careful but not with a friend.

Looking again at John, 15:13-14, you will notice that it doesn't come without a price. Obedience is required. Thus the lifestyle to develop in order to grow and establish one's position in the secret of God is strict adherence to the commands of the scriptures.

And those who obey the words written in the scriptures are automatically transformed into friends of God. That is, if you want to be His friend then you must love and practice His Word.

So, who are the friends of Jesus? They are those who do the things he commands:

> *"Jesus answered and said unto him, "if a man love Me, he will keep My words: and my Father will love him, and We will come unto him, and make our abode with him."* (John, 14:23)

Do you want to live with God? Then develop and maintain a lifestyle of practising the Word, for it will bring glory to God.

Chapter 4

Holy Spirit: Our Tour Guide

> *"For what a man knoweth the things of a man, except the spirit of man which is in him? Even so no man knoweth the things of God but the Spirit of God."* (1 Corinthians, 2:11).

No matter how you try, you cannot know the things of God without the Holy Spirit. Until you come to this realisation and understanding, you cannot make any progress concerning the Secret Place of God.

Therefore, we have to settle it in our hearts that we need the Holy Spirit to help us in our quest for the Secret Place: ". . . the things of God knoweth no man <u>but the Spirit of God</u>."

And I must tell you, nothing, absolutely nothing in the Christian faith will ever yield and results without the Holy Spirit. The Lord Himself said:

> *"I have yet many things to say unto you, but ye cannot bear them now. However when He, the Spirit of truth is come, He will guide you into all truth; for He shall not speak of Himself, but whatsoever He shall hear, that shall He speak: and He will show you things to come. He shall glorify Me; for He shall receive of Mine, and shall show it unto you. All things that the Father hath are Mine: therefore I said, that He shall take of Mine, and shall show it unto you."* (John, 16:12-15)

Emphasising this point is crucial. No man and no Christian can ever access the <u>things</u> of God without the Holy Spirit. Jesus said, "He will <u>guide you into all truth</u>." And if you compare or relate this verse with 1 Corinthians 2:11, you will see the same thoughts and message: "The things of God knoweth no man, but the Spirit of God."

So, in order to benefit fully and be well acquainted with God's Secret Place, the person and the ministry of the Holy Spirit, He is to be fully embraced. For instance, fellowship and prayers which are vital items in dwelling in God's presence, the man who is not filled in the Holy Ghost will find it quite boring. It takes the Holy Spirit to have an enjoyable and fruitful fellowship and prayer times with God (Romans, 8:26). It takes the Holy Spirit to overcome the infirmities men have in prayers.

Christ said, "When He, the Spirit of truth, is come, He will guide you into all truth." That is, the Holy Ghost is our tour guide and tutor in the truth which is also an important subject for dwelling in His presence.

And, according to scriptures, the truth is the Word of God. Without the person of the Holy Spirit, no Christian can know the truth of the Word. Why does the Bible seem like a chore for some seekers of the Secret Place of God? It is because they are not hungry enough to seek it. Let me relate this chapter in a clearer way. When you visit a historical site or a museum for the first time, you will find that there are usually tour guides to take people around, not only to guide them where to go but also to explain to them certain things that the visitors do not understand or know.

Those who have visited safari parks will attest to this fact. You see, without the tour guides, the safari and museum trips will be uninteresting, unproductive and possibly even dangerous. The same truth can be seen when seeking to abide with God. The Bible says, "O, the depth of the riches both of the wisdom and knowledge of God! How unsearchable are His judgements, and His ways past finding out." (Romans, 11:33)

The God we serve is a BIG God and HIS WAYS can never be fathomed by the minds and hearts of men. Therefore, they need someone who knows and understands it all. Who is this person? It is the Holy Spirit. (1 Corinthians, 2:11). The point is this, we need the Holy Spirit in order to have a fruitful journey in our desire to dwell with God. The devout Cornelius in Acts chapter 10, with all that he knew and did it was necessary for the great man of God, Peter, to administer salvation and the Holy Ghost baptism to him (Acts, 10:44-45). As a matter of fact, the angel who visited Cornelius to tell him of the need for Peter to visit him, said, ". . . call for one Simon whose name is Peter . . . he shall tell thee what thou oughtest to do." (Acts, 10:5-6)

From what happened when Peter visited Cornelius and his household we can see that what Cornelius 'ought to do' was firstly, to know Jesus as his personal saviour and not depend on the works of righteousness alone and, secondly, to receive the Holy Ghost with evidence of speaking in other tongues.

Now, if baptism and relationship with the Holy Ghost is one of the things Cornelius 'ought to do' that made God send an angel to the man, and also required such a great Apostle such as Peter to be pulled out of his ministerial duties to go visit a man, then the ministry of the Holy Ghost must be vital to any quest for a relationship with God. You cannot therefore make any progress in God's Secret Place with the Holy Spirit. He is the official tour guide.

Chapter 5

The Church and His Presence

Can any man be said to be dwelling in the Secret Place of God and not be an active lover and participator in the physical church of Christ on earth? Can a man be dwelling in God's presence and not be a church goer? Can you be living with God and not love the assembly of other children of God? In this chapter, we shall find out.

Let us begin by asking, 'What is the church and why the church?' and then we shall find out who instituted it. What is the church? The church is the body of Christ on earth. All Christians together form a living body, with Christ as the head of it:

> "*For as the body is one, and hath many members, and all the members of that one body, being many, are one body; so also is Christ. For by one spirit are we all baptised into one body, whether we be Jews or Gentiles . . . For the body is not one member, but many . . . But now hath God set the members each of them in the body, as it hath pleased Him . . . many members, yet but one body . . . Now ye are the body of Christ and members in particular.*" (1 Corinthians, 12:12-27).

> "*. . . so we, being, many, are one body in Christ, and every one members one of another.*" (Romans, 12:5)

> "*. . . and God hath put all things under His feet, and gave Him to be the head over all things to the church,*

which is His body the fullness of Him that filleth all in all." (Ephesians, 1:22-23).

The point I am trying to establish here is this, from the scriptures, the church is the symbolic representation of the body of Christ with Jesus as the head. That is the church. We are the body of Christ. It is a mystery but that is what it is: *"For we are members of His body, of His flesh, and of His bones . . . This is a great mystery . . ." (Ephesians, 5:30-32).*

As Christians, we are all joined to the body of Christ (Ephesians, 4:16), forming one body called the church. And just as the parts of the body of a man exist together, so does the body of Christ. None of the members of the body can live separately from each other.

"But now hath God set the members each of them in the body . . . And the eye cannot say unto the hand, I have

no need of thee." (1 Corinthians, 12:18-21)

From the above, it is necessary that any Christian who wants to dwell in God's Secret Place must pay particular attention to the body of Christ called the church. Why is this? It is because, in the body, every Christian is born into the kingdom. And in the body resides the presence of God on earth. And no Christian can be said to be in the spiritual body of Christ and not have association with it. How? Fellowshipping.

And fellowshipping is the reason of for the church. "God is faithful, by whom ye were called unto the fellowship of His son Jesus Christ our Lord." (1 Corinthians, 1:9).

> *"That which we have seen and heard, declare we unto you, that ye also may have fellowship with us: and truly our fellowship is with the Father, and with His Son Jesus Christ." (*1 John, 1:3)

In the fellowship of the church, God's presence is found. Every time the members of the body gather together, the Secret Place of God is in manifestation. So, those who want God's presence cannot keep away from the corporate body. The reason being is that God wants the unity of His children. Thus, He demonstrates, "Forsake not the assembly of yourselves together," (Hebrews, 10:25, paraphrased).

No Christian can ever survive outside of the church. It is just like a baby walking away from his or her mother and from the fellowship and care of the home and family.

If we say that we are children of God, then we require the care and shelter of God's home, if we are to survive the harsh weather of life and God's home on earth is the church: "But if I tarry long, that thou mayest know how thou ought to behave thyself in the house of God, which is the church of the living God, the pillar and ground of the truth." (1 Timothy, 3:15).

God's house on earth is the church. What a wonder that is. Therefore, to live in God's Secret Place is to be an active member of His church. No church membership and involvement equals no dwelling in God's Secret Place, no matter what anyone tries.

Who instituted the church? Jesus Christ our Lord instituted the church. He said, "I will build my church . . ." (Matthew, 16:18). And in instituting the church he gave it the highest authority.

In chapter 1, we mentioned that one of God's closets is the gathering ourselves together in His Name. And this is worth mentioning in this chapter also.

> *"For where two or three gather in My name, there am I in the midst of them."* (Matthew, 18:20).

It is God's design that His children gather together in His Name. And when such gathering is organised, God's presence is made manifest. The church and its gathering is God's command (Hebrews,

10:25), therefore, those who don't obey this command are in direct obedience to God and cannot except a private audience of God to be granted to them. Both rules must be obeyed: if you have private sessions with God in His presence, you must also have to cooperate with other Christians.

"The sceptre shall not depart from Judah, nor a lawgiver from between his feet, until Shiloh come; and unto Him shall the gathering of the people be." (Genesis, 49:10).

Chapter 6

Praise and the Secret Place

When you visit the house of a lawyer, you will see his law books; when you visit the house of a doctor, you are bound to see things such as a stethoscope; when you visit the house of a footballer, you will see medals, trophies and a football. So, when you go to the house of God what do you expect to see? Numerous things, in fact too many to mention but one thing you will not fail to see is praise and worship. God's house is filled and decorated with praise, worship and thanksgiving. As a matter of fact, praise is given constantly in Heaven. God is surrounded by praise and He is praised all day long.

> *". . . and, behold, a throne was set in Heaven, and One sat on the throne . . . And round about the throne were four and twenty seats . . . And before the throne there was a sea of glass like unto crystal: and in the midst of the throne, and round about the throne were four living beings full of eyes in front and behind.'*
>
> *'. . . And each of the four living beings had each of them six wings about him: and they were full of eyes within: and they rested not day and night, saying Holy, holy, holy, Lord God Almighty, who was and is and is to come."* (Revelation, 4:2-8)

Day and night there is praise and worship before God, and day and night they never cease to praise the living God.

So, one thing that is found commonly in God's house is praise. Music is constantly being expressed as a form of love and worship and adoration to Him. And so anyone who doesn't praise and worship cannot dwell with Him because praise is the lifestyle for His presence. It truly takes an attitude and a lifestyle of praise to live together with God.

Now, let us look at something very interesting about God and the beauty of praise:

> *"O My God, I cry in the daytime, but Thou hearest not; and in the night season, I am not silent. But thou art holy, O thou that inhabitest the praises of Israel."* (Psalms, 22:2-3)

In the above verses of the scriptures, David was trying to invite God's presence through his prayers and possibly through other ways; however, God could not be found. David did all he could "BUT THOU HEAREST NOT", was the only outcome and conclusion he could find. But we can see that the very moment David began to give God praise, He immediately came down. And from that personal and intimate experience, David came up with a new conclusion:

> *"But thou art holy, O thou that inhabitest the praises of Israel."* (Psalms, 22:3)

What is the lesson here? Yes, it is true that God is always with His people. It is true that God commands us to pray. But even though God is all around us, He only inhabits where the praises of His people are found. God will only live with those who give Him praise.

God's presence and dwelling is found in praise. When His people praise Him, they make him a dwelling place in their hearts. This truth is vital to those who want to live in the Secret Place of God. So, the first point to note concerning God and praise is this; God lives in praise and this is what we have seen in Psalms 22:3 as well as Revelation, chapters four and five. Therefore, if you are not a praise person, you cannot live with God because He lives in the praise of His people; if you want to live with God then you must be ready to praise Him.

The second point to note is this: it takes praise, worship and thanksgiving to enter into God's dwelling place. That is, even though you are invited, until you give Him praise, you will not be allowed in.

> *"Enter into His gates with thanksgiving and into His courts with praise, Be thankful unto Him, and bless His Name."* (Psalms, 100:4)

We can only go through the gates of Heaven and enter into the dwelling place of God through praise. From all the above, we have learnt an important and vital secret, the password to dwell with God, it is through praise. And to dwell with Him even after you have been let in, a continuous, never-ending praise is a must.

If you love the things that God loves, then you will dwell with Him. And what is it that God loves? God loves praise. And how do you find out what a man loves? By the way he or she reacts. Flick through the pages of the ancient scriptures and you will see that our God loves praise. Any time God is praised, He works wondrous miracles:

> *"And when they began to sing and to praise, the Lord set ambushments against the children of Ammon, Moab, and Mount Seir, who had come against Judah and they were smitten."* (2 Chronicles, 20:22)

Chapter 7

Benefits of the Secret Place of God

To describe what a man stands to gain by dwelling in the Secret Place of God is like going to the seashore and counting all the grains of sand. Is that possible? I believe not. That is the amount of blessings, the extent of power and anointing you will gain, too much for the human mind to comprehend.

The benefits of the Secret Place of God is just simply all about God. No one can ever exhaust what you stand to gain by dwelling with God. If we are to count all the blessings, we will never end (Psalms, 139:17-18). You can live life a hundred times over and I guarantee that you will still be counting the blessings of the dwelling place of God.

"He that dwelleth in the secret place of the most high, shall abide under the shadow of the Almighty; I will say of the Lord he is my refuge and my fortress: my God in Him will I trust.

Surely He shall deliver thee from the snare of the fowler and from the noisome pestilence. He shall cover thee with His feathers, and under His wings shalt thou trust; His truth shall be thy shield and buckler. Thou shalt not be afraid of the terror by night, nor of the arrows that flieth by day, nor of the pestilence that walketh in darkness; nor of the destruction that layeth waste at noonday. A thousand shall fall at thy side, and ten thousand at thy right hand, but it shall not come nigh thee. Only with thine eyes shalt thou behold and see the reward of the wicked.

Because thou hast made the Lord who is my refuge, even the Most High thy inhabitation; there shall no evil befall thee, neither shall any plague come nigh thy dwelling. For He shall give His angels charge over thee, to keep thee in all thy ways. They shall bear thee up in their hands, lest thou dash thy foot against a stone. Thou shalt tread upon the lion and adder: the young lion and the dragon shalt thou trample under foot.

Because he hath set his love upon Me, therefore will I deliver him: I will set him on high, because he hath known My name. He shall call upon Me and I will answer him: I will be with him in trouble, I will deliver him, and honour him. With long life *will I satisfy him and show him My salvation." (*Psalms, 91:1-16)

What a remarkable scripture! Did you see all that? Amazing is it not? Just for obeying verse one, all the rest becomes yours. Notice that verses 9 and 14 are very insightful. They give the reasons why God would do all that is stated in the other verses for you. In fact, these two verses give more meaning to what it means to dwell in the Secret Place of God.

"Because thou hast made the Lord, which is my refuge, even the most high, thy habitation . . . because he [you] hath set his [your] love upon Me . . . because he [you] hath known My name." (Psalms, 91: 9,14).

That is, to dwell in God's Secret Place is to make him your HABITATION, and what will be the benefits?

1. Deliverance from the snare of the fowler. That is, no plan of the enemy will ever succeed over you. You will always come out victorious no matter what the devil's traps.

2. Deliverance from noisome pestilence, no matter how loud the pestilence in the world are, you will be free.

3. Total protection from evil and harm; "He shall cover thee with his feathers" (verse 4).

4. If you are truly a dweller in His presence, spiritual boldness shall be your portion. Verse five says, "Thou shalt not be afraid for the terror or for the arrows, of pestilence nor for destruction." Those who dwell in God's Secret Place are so bold that they scare away evil.

5. Household insurance is the blessing for those who dwell with God: "There

shall no evil befall thee, neither shall any plague come nigh thy dwelling" (verse 10).

6. Angelic protection and ministration is another benefit; "For he shall give his angels charge over thee . . ." (verse 11).

7. Victorious life and promotion.

8. "He shall call upon me, and I will answer him . . .", those who dwell with God will always experience answers to their prayers.

9. "With long life will I satisfy him and show him my salvation" (verse 16). Check with those who lived with God and you will discover that they all experienced long life.

Do you want to live an enviable life on earth? Then living with God is the greatest secret in gaining it. Men are in defeat, despair and disgrace because they are far from God. Make God your dwelling place and a life of honour will be your inheritance.